Collins Engl

GH00888642

Series editors: K R Cripwell ar

A library of graded readers for
language, and for reluctant na
levels of difficulty. Structure, v
all controlled according to principles laid down in detail in A Guide to
Collins English Library. A list of the books follows. Numbers after each
title indicate the level at which the book is written: 1 has a basic
vocabulary of 300 words and appropriate structures, 2 : 600 words, 3 :
1000 words, 4 : 1500 words, 5 : 2000 words and 6 : 2500 words.

Collins English Library Level 2

THE STORY OF
SCOTLAND YARD

Lewis Jones

Collins ELT

Printed by Martin's of Berwick
Published in Great Britain by
William Collins Sons and Co Ltd
Glasgow G4 0NB

First published in Collins English Library 1983
Reprinted: 1985, 1987, 1989

ISBN 00 370151 4

We are grateful to the Central Office of Information and
the Home Office for permission to reproduce the
photograph which appears on the cover. For permission to
reproduce the text photographs, we would like to thank the
following, Central Office of Information(p6), Fox Photos
Ltd. (p22) and the Publicity Branch of New Scotland Yard
(pp8, 11, 13, 14, 16, 23, 28, 30, 33, 36).

Cover design by Dan Lim

The publishers are grateful to the Public Information
Department at New Scotland Yard for their help in
checking the facts in this book.

Contents

How it began

200 years ago, there were no policemen in Britain. The streets of London were very dangerous. Thieves worked openly in daylight. When people ran after a thief, his friends used knives and swords and guns, and helped him to escape.

Some of the richest places in London were the ships on the River Thames. These ships brought treasures from all parts of the world. And at night, thieves carried away many of those treasures— and sometimes parts of the ships.

So about 60 men got together, and became the River Police. They carried swords, and they went up and down the Thames in small boats. They did a good job, and soon there were a few policemen on the streets of London too.

Some rode on horseback, and some went about on foot. They wore blue and red clothes, and a tall black hat. And they carried a gun, a sword, and a heavy stick. But there were very few of them for a city of $1\frac{1}{2}$ million people.

Then, on 30 September 1829, for the first time, London got its first real police. They carried a heavy stick, and a light at night. More than 3000 men became policemen, and they worked from a big house at 4 Whitehall Place—not far from the Houses of Parliament. Most of the policemen used

4, Whitehall Place – the old Scotland Yard

the door at the back of the house, and that came out in Scotland Yard.

Soon, people began to use the name for the home of the new police. That home has now moved to a different building. But the new building still keeps its old name—Scotland Yard.

London and the City

Since those early days, some other things have not changed. There's a small part of London that's called the City of London. It's really the business centre: the Bank of England is there, and the head offices of other big banks.

People come there to work in offices during the

mornings and afternoons, but in the evenings and at weekends, the streets are quiet.

If you stand at the centre, you can walk about 1 kilometre and be out of the City.

When London got its first police, the City didn't want them. A few years later, the City got its own police. And it's still the same today.

But when people talk of 'London', they mean Greater London, with its 7 million people. If you stand at its centre, you must walk about 25 kilometres to leave it. About 26 000 policemen and policewomen work in it.

Looking at Policemen

Before 1829, when there was trouble in the streets, the army arrived to stop it. But the army's job was killing enemies. Many soldiers didn't want to fight against their own townspeople. But in the streets of their own country, they often hurt too many people.

Once in the town of Manchester, 60 000 people arrived to hear a famous speaker. Soldiers on horseback came to take him away. But before the end of the day, they killed 11 of the listeners, and badly wounded 400 others.

So people were afraid when they heard about

the new 'policemen'. They thought these men would be street-soldiers.

So the first police tried to be different from the army. The army was famous for its bright red clothes. So the London police wore dark blue coats. Soldiers carried guns. So the police didn't wear any. It's still the same today.

The City police wanted to be different from the others, so they wore their own kind of clothes. Today you can still know a City policeman by his clothes. Some things (like his hat) are a little different.

London's first police did a good job, and thieves and people like them began to leave for other towns. These towns soon had a difficult time, because the only police in the country were in London.

Over the next 20 or 30 years, other parts of Britain began to have their own police. But they did it in their own time, and in their own way. Today, the 43 different parts of Britain still each have their own police. They don't dress very differently from London policemen, but some things (hats again) are not the same.

You can see something of the story of Britain's police in their clothes.

This is how London policemen and women dress today. Look at the photograph on page 6 and see how much police clothes have changed in the last 90 years.

The Yard

New Scotland Yard is still at the heart of London's police. And today, many people just call it 'the Yard'. But not many of London's 26 000 police work there.

About 2000 policemen work in the building, and about 6000 people who are not in the police. So only a quarter of the people at the Yard are police.

They deal with about 5000 telephone calls every hour, and they get 2000 letters every day. Their work begins at 7.30 every morning, when the post arrives. Twice each day, 31 bags of police mail arrive from other parts of London. Radio calls (not always in English) come from all over the world.

Different parts of the Yard—different departments—deal with different things. One department gives out policemen's pay. People in other departments are buying cars and motorbikes. Others are dealing with new tables and chairs and desks, or meals.

Department D has the job of finding new policemen.

Learning the Job

1 out of every 5 people in England lives in London. And 1 out of every 4 policemen in England lives in London. So Scotland Yard is always looking for new policemen and policewomen.

They can begin the job if they're between $18\frac{1}{2}$ and 30. Men must be over 172 centimetres tall, and women over 168 centimetres.

New Scotland Yard has its own police school at the Peel Centre at Hendon, in the northwest of London. When a man wants to become a policeman, he first goes to Hendon for 5 months. He lives in rooms at the school, and he can use its sports fields. There are classrooms at Hendon, but he won't be at a desk all the time.

New policemen and women working hard at Hendon

He learns about police work outside. He learns how to help people who are hurt. He learns about car thieves, and troubles on the road. And he must learn about London—it's going to be his place of work for a long time. He learns to swim, and to save lives in the water.

After Hendon, he moves to a police station. For the first two weeks, the beginner goes around with another policeman from the station. He must learn about that part of London, and about some of the people who live and work there. After that, he can perhaps start to work alone in the streets.

During the next months, he goes on learning. He spends two days in every month at a learning centre. He spends some time in different kinds of police work (we'll look at some of them later in the book).

Learning the job on the streets of London

Then, after two years, if he's good at the job, he becomes a real policeman.

Men and women go through the same lessons at the Hendon police school. And when they begin real police work, women do the same jobs as men, and they get the same pay.

New Scotland Yard's Department A deals with policemen and policewomen. Some of these men and women like to go on and do different police jobs. But most of them enjoy working at a police station, and they stay there.

The Police Station

The police have cut London into four quarters. And they've cut each quarter into 6 parts. So for the police, London is a town in 24 big pieces. Each of these pieces is called by a different letter.

New Scotland Yard is in piece A. The biggest police station in each piece of London also uses the letter D. So the biggest station in piece H is called HD.

London has 185 police stations, large and small. The smallest of them all is on a traffic island in the middle of the road, at Hyde Park Corner. Thousands of car drivers pass it every day, but very few Londoners know it's there. And on the

The only floating police station in the world

River Thames, at Waterloo, there's the only police station that floats on water.

Some of the small stations are closed at night, but the bigger ones are open 24 hours a day. If you go into one of them, you'll first meet a policeman at a desk.

Perhaps you've found a dog (the police will keep it for a week, while they wait for its owner). Perhaps a thief has run off with your money. Perhaps you've lost your car. Maybe *you* are lost. The policeman at the desk is there to help you.

In another room at the station, people are working with radios and telephones. Suppose the police get the man who took your money. They'll put him in a cell—a police station has a number of these rooms with strong doors.

Maybe the station will have a games room, a reading-room, and a room like a small restaurant, where policemen and women can eat their meals.

There'll also be rooms for the detectives—the men and women who wear their own clothes, not the dark blue police clothes.

Detectives

London's police began (you remember) back in 1829. At that time, people wanted policemen to wear police clothes. People in the street wanted to *know* who was a policeman and who wasn't. So they didn't much like the thought of detectives. People thought they could be spies. That's why it was another 12 years before the first detectives arrived.

The new Detective Department had 6 of them. Today, about 3300 men and women detectives work in the streets of London. Most of them work from police stations.

Before a man can become a detective, he must spend two years as a policeman first. Then he'll go to the Detective Department of the police school at Hendon. There, they learn to use their eyes.

Sometimes, in a class, a visitor will come in and sit down. After a while, he'll get up and quietly leave. Half an hour later, the people in the class must suddenly answer some questions:

"Did you see a visitor? Where did he sit? How long did he stay? About how old was he? How tall? What colour was his hair? Was he fat or thin? What did he do? What shape was his mouth? Do you remember his face? His ears? His nose? What was his eye-colour?

"Did he wear a coat? What kind of coat? What else did he wear? Suppose we want that man, and we must radio to all parts of the country about him. What can you tell us about him? How much did you see? Can you remember enough?"

When a thief takes something, he'll want to sell it for money. But before he can do that, he'll perhaps hide it. A beginner-detective must learn to find it. Small things (like tickets for a big football game) are perhaps inside his clothes. Bigger things, like gold spoons or plates, could be in his room. How many hiding-places are there in a house? A detective must learn where they are. And he must know the possible hiding-places in a car or lorry.

A policeman hopes to stop trouble before it begins. But if it still happens, detectives move in, and try to get some answers: "Who is the thief?" "Where is the money now?" "Who killed this man?" "How did he get into the house?" "Did some person see him?" "Where can we find him?"

It could take months before detectives get answers to their questions.

Department C at New Scotland Yard has its own detectives. Some of them try to find cars. When thieves take a car, they often try to change its looks—its colour, its number, its different parts. And sometimes they put the parts of different cars together, to make a 'new' car. Car detectives look hard for these kinds of change.

When there's a killing on a British ship at sea, who goes and deals with it? Detectives from New Scotland Yard. They're ready for work day and night. And not only in London—police in other parts of Britain can ask for their help.

The police of more than a hundred different countries work together in Interpol. Each country in Interpol passes police news to others who ask for it. At the Yard, Department C deals with the work of Interpol. And there's always a Yard man at Interpol's head office in Paris.

If George Smith from the north of England gets into trouble with the French police, they can soon learn more about him from Scotland Yard. Today, a killer or a thief can sometimes reach another country very fast. But radio news by Interpol moves faster. And the man could walk off his plane into the arms of detectives.

A detective's job is mostly long, hard work. They often see a lot of people and ask a lot of questions. But sometimes the answers are not enough, and the police turn to science.

Fingerprints

On a Monday morning in March of 1905, the police found an old man dead in his kitchen. His name was Mr Farrow, and he lived behind his oil shop in south London. Some person hit the old man over the head and killed him.

On Mondays, Mr Farrow had all of the shop's money for the past week. The police found his money-box, but the money was gone.

A few people saw two men near the shop early that morning. Later, the police took two brothers to the police station. But were the Stratton brothers the killers? When the Strattons went to court, people said different things. Some thought the Strattons were the men near the shop. Others only said, "Perhaps". Then the court called for Inspector Collins. He was the fingerprint man from New Scotland Yard.

"Every one of us is different," he said. "And each one of us arrives in this world with finger-ends that are different. At New Scotland Yard, I have worked with fingerprints for 10 years. And I have never found two fingerprints the same.

"The fingerprints of two different men are different in many ways. I have never found more than three points that are the same. More than that—prints from different fingers of the same person are not the same either."

Then the Inspector showed the court a small box. "This is the money-box from Mr Farrow's oil shop," he said. "And here, on this shiny black part of the box, I found a fingerprint. Now I'd like you to look at these pictures."

Inspector Collins showed a picture of the print from the box. He also showed pictures of a fingerprint from Alfred Stratton. He talked for a long time about the many points that were the same.

The question for the court was: "Did Alfred Stratton ever touch the old man's money-box?" And later, the court gave its answer: "Yes". They now believed that the Stratton brothers killed old Mr Farrow. It was the first time that fingerprints led to a killer.

At the beginning, the Yard had only three fingerprint men. Today, 425 people work with fingerprints in Department B.

When the courts send a man or woman to prison, that person's fingerprints go to New Scotland Yard. But if the courts let a person go free, the police burn the fingerprints.

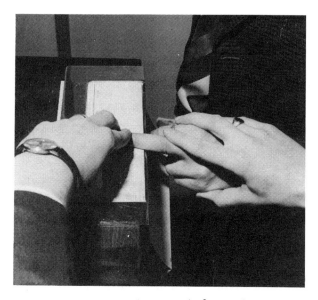

A policeman takes a man's fingerprints

Perhaps a stranger has broken into your house, and you call the police. Maybe they will take fingerprints. Some of those prints will perhaps be yours, and others could belong to your family and friends. What happens to those fingerprints? The police burn them.

New Scotland Yard now has the fingerprints of more than 2 million people. And police from all over Britain can find out about them from the Police National Computer at Hendon.

Suppose Bill Harker goes to prison in a town in the west of England. His fingerprints go to the

A policeman looking for fingerprints on a car door

Police National Computer. Perhaps a few years later, Gus Wilson breaks into a house in Manchester, and he also goes to prison. But the computer says that his fingerprints are the prints of Bill Harker. This is the same man, and he's changed his name.

Again, suppose a man breaks into a house, and leaves his fingerprint on a window in the city of Liverpool. Perhaps the computer has never met this print before, so it can't help. But it doesn't forget this print—it keeps it.

Later, perhaps the same print arrives again—at other times and from other places. The computer remembers them all.

Then one day the police get a thief in a little market town. His fingerprints go to the computer, and it's met these prints before, a number of times. The first time was from a window in Liverpool. Now the man must find some answers about a number of break-ins, not just one.

Often, just part of a fingerprint is enough. Or a print from some other part of the hand. But sometimes there are no fingerprints. Then the police can turn to more of their scientists for help.

Science

Police scientists don't work inside New Scotland Yard. They have their own building on the other side of the River Thames, and about 200 of them work there. They ask two questions most often. One of these questions is: "What is it?"

The police find a dead body in the Thames. It's been there for a few months. There's a name inside the coat, but now the eye can't read it—it's been in the water too long. What name is it? The scientists put it under ultra-violet light, then they can see the name again.

Before an old man dies, perhaps he wrote: '*I leave all my money to Mr Donaldson.*' Or did he? After he's dead, his family can't believe that he wrote that. They ask the police for help, and the scientists use their ultra-violet light again.

Under the name *Mr Donaldson*, they find the words *my dear son*. Some person has changed the old man's words. Now perhaps the police will have some questions for Mr Donaldson.

A man dies strangely and suddenly after a meal. Did something in his food kill him? The police scientists try to find answers.

Sometimes, answers bring new questions, and scientists and police between them look for new answers:

What is on this man's shoes? Sand. Where is it from? Where has he been? ...

What's the dark colour on the front of this shirt? Coffee? Milk? Tea? Oil? No, it's blood. Whose is it? How did it get there? ...

Is this a little piece of cloth? No, it's a hair. From a man or a woman? Neither—it's from an animal. What kind of animal? A cat. Did this man own a cat? No. Did the dead person have a cat? Yes. What colour? Light brown. Could this hair be from the cat? Yes. But this man says he didn't go into the house—how did he get the cat's hair on his trousers? ...

What are these little pieces on this man's clothes? Very small bits of glass. Did the killer break any glass? Yes, he stood outside a shop window, and shot through it at the owner inside.

The second question that police scientists ask most often is this: "Are these two things the same?"

A man shot at the owner of an office, then escaped. He didn't hit the owner, and the bullet went into the office wall. Detectives took the bullet out of the wall. And they didn't forget it—they kept it.

Two years later, the police wanted another man for a different job. They found him, and the man had a gun. Police scientists shot the gun, then took a hard look at the bullet. They also got the bullet from two years before, and looked at that again. The two bullets came from the same gun. Now the man was in trouble for both jobs ...

A man killed a young housewife with a knife and escaped. She wore a light red dress. When the police found a possible killer, they gave his clothes to the scientists. There were 61 small bits of light red cloth on the man's coat, and 22 more on his hat. It was the same kind of cloth as the woman's dress.

But that was not enough. When the police looked in the side pocket of the man's car, they found a little dry blood in the bottom corner. The scientists asked, "Is this the same kind of blood as the young housewife's?" They found that it was.

One day a car hit a man on a bike and killed him. The car driver didn't stop. Later, the police found a little piece of something black in the road. The scientists told them that it came from a car. The car, they said, was black when it was new. Over the years, the owner changed the colour three times—and the last colour was black again.

Then a policeman remembered a driver who often hit things, and then put new colours on his car. The police visited the man, and they took a small black piece from near the front of his car. When this car was new, it was black. It had three changes of colour. Then it was black again ...

Sometimes the work of the scientists can keep people *out* of trouble. One night, a woman telephoned the police. "A lorry has just hit a child," she said. "I saw him. Then he stopped, and put the child's body in the back of his lorry. Then he drove off."

The police went to the road and found some blood. Then they began to look for a lorry driver with a dead child in the back of his lorry.

But the scientists told them, "Forget it. We've looked at the blood, and it's from an animal—a cow. We think the lorry hit a young cow. The driver didn't want a fight with an angry farmer, so he took the body away with him. In the dark, the woman thought the small animal was a child."

Horses

The police have used horses almost from the beginning. In London today, you can often see police horses when a great many people come together in the streets. It's often for a very important happening.

Scotland Yard's Department A deals with police on horseback. A man on horseback is high up, and he can look over people's heads. When the streets are full, he can still see trouble a long way off. In the country, a horseman can leave the roads, and cross fields and move through trees.

Police on horseback with some football fans

Policemen and women must spend two years at a police station before they can work with horses. Often they've never worked with horses before. But after 22 weeks at Imber Court, on the west side of London, they can ride horses and work with them.

Most of the horses are from Yorkshire, in the north of England, and they arrive when they're 3 or 4 years old. If you know a horse's name, you know when the police bought him—the first letter of his name tells you the year. The letter H means 1979, the letter I means 1980 ...

A police horse must often work in the middle of noise and people and cars. So he must learn not to be afraid of these things. While he enjoys his food, his teachers move around and make a lot of noise. Later, he hears the sounds of guns and railway trains and big football matches and heavy traffic. He also learns not to be afraid of large numbers of angry people. He learns to move *sideways* into people, when his rider wants to move them along.

After six months, he's ready. He's not afraid of loud, sudden noises any more. When you see the queen on horseback, she's riding a police horse.

Each horse goes on working for about 14 years. The police now have about 200 horses. But these are not the only animals that help them.

Dogs

Scotland Yard first began to try dogs in 1946. By the end of that year, it still had only 6. Today more than 300 police dogs are working in London.

When a young dog is 3 months old, it goes to the home of a policeman or policewoman. From then, this person will be the dog's 'handler'. The dog stays at his handler's home, lives with his family, plays with the children. A handler must learn to really know his dog.

When the dog is 9 months old, he goes with his handler for a week to the police dog school at

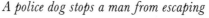

A police dog stops a man from escaping

Keston, in the south of London. When the dog is a year old, it begins about 12 weeks of lessons in police work.

It learns to follow a person's smell along the ground. It learns to look for people in buildings, and in open country. It learns to find things that are lost.

It runs after a man if its handler tells it. When the man stops, the dog will also stop and stay with him—nothing else. But if the man kicks or tries to escape, the dog will take the man's arm in its mouth. Always the right arm, because most people use their right hands. The dog won't bite or try to hurt the man. But it will hold him while it waits for the handler to arrive.

Traffic

London has 14 000 kilometres of roads, and on every kilometre there are 180 cars and buses and taxis and lorries. That's why there are more than a thousand men and women in London's traffic police.

Every day, they must deal with about $2\frac{1}{2}$ million cars and lorries and bikes. Their job is to see that London's traffic moves along easily and safely, day and night.

Some years ago, the traffic in London became very heavy at two times of the day. Once in the morning, when people left home and went to work; and once more in the late afternoon, when people finished work, and were on their way home again. But today, there's not much difference between those hours and the other times of the day.

Lorries take things in and out of London all day long. Cars and buses and taxis are always on the move. There are times when traffic becomes very thick—and sometimes everything just stops.

Perhaps a car has hit another. Perhaps a heavy lorry has broken down—and in some places, that can bring part of London to a stop. Or perhaps some traffic lights are not working. When this kind of thing happens, the traffic police will soon be there to help.

How do the police know where there's trouble? Scotland Yard's computer knows when any one of a thousand traffic lights isn't working. And when cars are moving too slowly, the computer can change the timing of traffic lights.

There are television eyes on the top of some tall buildings. These give a picture of London's traffic. And at the traffic centre, a policeman sits in front of a television and looks for trouble. If the traffic in one place is becoming too thick, he sends traffic police there.

The traffic centre – police look for trouble

The traffic police have their own cars, of course, but the traffic centre doesn't send these. It sends police on motorbikes. When cars have all stopped, the bikes can still move in and out of the spaces in traffic.

Police on motorbikes soon arrive at the place in trouble, and at other places nearby. Each traffic policeman can talk to the others and to the traffic centre by radio. Perhaps the police will send some of the cars along emptier streets, and soon the traffic will begin to move again.

Sometimes a big lorry is carrying something that's very wide—some of these things can be over 30 metres long, and as much as 400 tons. The driver asks for help, and police motorbikes will drive ahead of the lorry and behind it. They'll keep other traffic away from the lorry, and out of danger.

Sometimes people get hurt—a car driver perhaps, or a girl on a bike, or a man on foot. Traffic police know how to help. And they can use their radios to get more help. Perhaps they'll ask for an ambulance for the person who's hurt. In very heavy traffic, the police will help the ambulance to get through.

In London, you can hear the traffic centre on your own radio. You know you're listening to the traffic centre when you hear the name 'Oscar'. The centre uses the name Oscar when it's talking to its traffic police around London.

The centre also sends news of the traffic to London's radio stations. So London car drivers can turn on their radios when they want the latest news of the traffic ahead of them.

River Police

The motor boats of the River Police move up and down the Thames 24 hours a day. They deal with 85 kilometres of the river, and they work from 3 police stations. The one at Waterloo is not just the only floating police station in London, but the only one in the world.

The river police fight fires on ships, and in the buildings on land nearby. They bring back boats that float away from the land and become a danger. And they deal with any ship that hits another. They save people who've fallen into the river—a number of people now use the Thames for water sports.

Sometimes people try to lose things in the river. A killer will perhaps go to one of London's bridges, and drop his gun into the water. A thief perhaps learns that the police know all about his latest job. Where can he hide the suitcase full of money? Maybe at the bottom of the Thames.

There are 9 'frogmen' in the river police. Their job is to look for things—and people—under water.

What do you think these frogmen are looking for? →

999

If you want police help when you're in London, telephone 999. People call that number when they want police, or an ambulance, or firemen.

Your call won't reach the police at first. It will only get as far as the telephone company. The telephone people know that a 999 caller wants help, and a voice will ask you what kind. Answer, "Police", and your call will now go through to New Scotland Yard.

Why does the telephone company take your call before the police get it? Callers are sometimes hurt, or ill. Sometimes they begin a call but they can't finish it. Perhaps they can't talk.

Maybe some other person takes the telephone from them, and puts it down again—then New Scotland Yard alone can't help. They don't know where the caller is, and they can't find out. But the telephone people can. They can find out the telephone number, and then the place. Then they'll tell the police, and a police car will soon be on its way.

Perhaps you wake up in the middle of the night. You think you can hear a thief in the house. You call 999 and ask for the police. Then you look around the house and find that nothing is wrong. You telephone 999 again, and tell the police, "It's all right. I was wrong. I don't want the police now."

But a police car will still arrive. Was it really you who made that second call? Or did a thief make it, and try to stop the police? The police will want to know. So they'll come round and ask you.

What happens when your 999 call gets through to New Scotland Yard? It arrives at a long room. 24 men and women are ready to take the calls. In front of each one, there's something like a television. When your call comes through, it goes to the next person who's free.

He listens to what you say. His fingers touch the letters in front of him, and the words come up in green letters on the television. If he wants to send a police car to you, the words will also come up on a radio man's television.

A computer also puts on to this television some fast answers to questions: Where is the caller? Which cars are free to answer this call? Where are they?

The whole thing takes only seconds.

The Police National Computer

Police in all parts of Britain can make use of the Police National Computer. It can answer many of their questions very fast.

In the days before computers, the police could stop a car and question the driver. Sometimes he said he was the owner. But was he? Often a policeman asked, "What's the number of this car?" The owner would know, but a thief somtimes didn't remember.

There were other possible questions: "How many kilometres has this car done since new?" "What's in the back of the car?"

The police could radio and ask for the latest news about the car. And New Scotland Yard would look through their cards. All this could take 10 minutes or more.

Suppose a thief takes your car in London today. You tell the police, and they tell the police computer. Perhaps a policeman in a car sees your car ahead of him in traffic. He radios the number of your car to New Scotland Yard, and in seconds the Yard's computer can tell him the latest news.

Have you (the owner) got your car back yet? Or is it the thief who's driving it now? The policeman has the answer before he gets out his car. When he gets the man's name, he can radio that to the Yard too. Maybe the computer will know something else about the man. Perhaps he's driven dangerously in the past, and the courts won't let him drive again. The police computer knows the names of people who mustn't drive.

At any time, the police want a number of

people—the computer knows their names too. The computer even knows about fingerprints. It remembers fingerprints, and it can answer questions about them. It also shows television pictures of them.

The Machine at Work

Here is a story that could happen. It shows how the police machine works.

One summer night, two men broke into some houses in a quiet street. They wanted radios and televisions. They made very little noise. But at the last house, they broke the kitchen window.

There was a woman alone in the house. She woke up when she heard the breaking of glass. She went quietly downstairs to the telephone in the dining room. She called 999, and gave her number. Then she turned and saw a man in the door. In his hand was a long kitchen knife.

"Put it down," he said.

The voice on the phone asked, "What's the trouble?"

The woman kept her eyes on the knife, and said, "It's all right. I don't want any help, thank you. Good night." Then she put the phone down.

The second man came in with a piece of wood

in his hand. He said, "Come on. This television's heavy. I want some help."

His friend said, "We haven't time for it now. When we go, she'll 'phone the police."

"Oh no, she won't," said the second man, and he hit the woman with the heavy piece of wood. She fell to the floor and was still.

The two men went back to the living room, and carried the television out to a dark blue car outside. Then they jumped in and drove off fast without any lights.

A few streets away, a policewoman saw the car with no lights. But she couldn't see the number. She spoke into her personal radio.

A few minutes later, the woman on the dining-room floor began to wake up, and she heard a man's voice. She was suddenly afraid again, but then the light came on and a policeman walked in.

"Your kitchen door was open," he said. "Are you all right?"

He helped her to stand, and through the window she saw a police car outside.

"How did you know where to come?" she asked.

"You gave your number to the telephone people, remember? They told us where you lived. What's happened?"

She told him. Her head still hurt badly, and the policeman 'phoned for an ambulance. Then two detectives arrived, and another man who looked for fingerprints and the piece of wood.

By now the two men drove along more slowly, with their lights on. Just out of town, they went past a traffic police car at the roadside. There was nothing wrong about the dark blue car. But the two traffic policemen knew about the break-in from their radio. Also, it was the middle of the night, with nearly empty roads.

The police driver thought he would follow the dark blue car for a while, and the man beside him radioed the car's number. At New Scotland Yard, a man gave the number to the police computer.

In a few seconds, the television in front of him gave him the news—the day before, a man gave that same number to the police. He told them, "It's the number of my car. It's gone from outside my office."

The man at the Yard radioed this to the men in the police car. They turned on the big blue light on top of their car, and began a fast drive after the other car. But the thieves only went faster.

In a small country road, the police car passed the dark blue car and suddenly turned in front of it. The two thieves jumped out and ran across a field. As the two policemen got out of their car, they saw a long kitchen knife in the hands of one of the men. The policemen made a short radio call and ran after the two men.

The men ran through a wood and along the side

of a river. One of them dropped the knife into the water.

By now, a police dog handler was on the way. When he reached the cars at the roadside, he let the dog follow the smell of the men. At a small bridge, the traffic police already had one man.

"The other one got away," they called.

The dog led his handler over a bridge, into an empty farmhouse, and up some stairs. The man was in one of the upstairs rooms. When he saw the dog, he stood still and didn't try to escape.

At daylight, two police frogmen went into the river (they don't only work on the Thames). They soon found the kitchen knife and brought it up. In the dark blue car there were four televisions. And the police computer looked at the fingerprints and named the two men. They'd been in trouble with the police before.

Without cars and radios and computers, the machine that is Scotland Yard would work much more slowly. But without the policemen and policewomen on the streets, and the detectives, and the scientists, and the dog handlers, and the frogmen, and the traffic police and many others, the machine would not work at all.

The men and women who work for Scotland Yard *are* the machine.

A Word Game

Here are 68 questions for you. All the answers are from the book.

Write down the first letter of every answer. These 68 letters make a sentence—it's from a British writer of about 130 years ago.

The sentence is about the police. Do you think it's true?

1   Where is Interpol's head office?
2   The River Police deal with ships that are
    _____ fire.
3   Detectives often ask a _____ of questions.
4   If the police bought a horse in 1980, its
    name begins with the letter _____.
5   Which department tries to find cars?
6   People's fingerprints are all different:
    prints from the same person are not the same,
    _____.
7   Traffic police ride on them.
8   Television _____ watch London's traffic.
9   The telephone company can tell the police
    your phone _____.
10 It carries away people who are hurt.
11 Frogmen don't only work on the _____
    Thames.

44

12 Scotland Yard had only 6 dogs by the _____ of 1946.
13 How do police horses move into people?
14 The traffic centre uses this name on the radio.
15 The Yard's computer knows about the working of a thousand traffic _____.
16 Police who wear their own clothes.
17 The police of many countries work together here.
18 At some stations, the police can _____ in their own restaurant.
19 A police car can ask for computer help by _____.
20 Most police work at a police _____.
21 The only police station that floats on water.
22 London's police have about 200 of these animals.
23 A policeman _____ horseback can see a long way.
24 Which department deals with horses?
25 A room with strong doors at a police station.
26 How many police stations do the River Police have?
27 A police dog holds a man's right _____.
28 Where were Britain's first police?
29 People come to the City to work in _____.
30 Telephone this number for police help.
31 You must be _____ years old before you can become a British policeman.

32 Scotland Yard is in part _____ of London.

33 Most police horses come from the _____ of England.

34 In each part of London, the biggest police station uses this letter.

35 It was at the back of 4 Whitehall Place.

36 You can hear the traffic centre _____ the radio.

37 Each part of London is called by a different _____.

38 Which department finds new policemen?

39 London's smallest police station is on a traffic _____.

40 On London's streets 200 years ago, a thief's friends helped him to _____.

41 The queen sometimes _____ on a police horse.

42 How many men were in the first River Police?

43 When there were no police, the _____ dealt with trouble in the streets.

44 Soldiers' clothes were bright _____.

45 Work at the Yard begins at 7.30 _____ morning.

46 Only a quarter of the people at the Yard are _____.

47 Police horses must not be afraid _____ noise.

48 Every policeman must _____ to swim.

49 You can't become a British policeman _____ you're over 30.

50 The Police National _____ is at Hendon.

51 _____ part of Britain has its own police.

52 _____ and women get the same police pay.

53 When did London get its first real police?

54 Thieves sometimes try to make a _____ car from different parts.

55 Who must be 160 centimetres tall in the police?

56 A policeman who works with a dog.

57 What did Mr Farrow sell?

58 200 years _____, Britain had no police.

59 The business centre of London.

60 The police have cut London into a number of parts; how many?

61 A beginner becomes a real policeman after _____ years.

62 Scotland Yard is more than 150 years _____.

63 Soldiers carry them, but British police don't.

64 Many people thought the first police were _____, not friends.

65 How many policemen and women work in London?

66 Where is the police school (Peel Centre)?

67 The City is quiet in the _____ and at weekends.

68 The _____ Police use motor boats.

1 Paris **2** on **3** lot **4** "I" **5** "C" **6** either
7 motorbikes **8** eyes **9** number **10** ambulance
11 River **12** end **13** sideways **14** Oscar **15** lights
16 detectives **17** Interpol **18** eat **19** radio
20 station **21** Waterloo **22** horses **23** on **24** "A"
25 cell **26** three **27** arm **28** London **29** offices
30 "999" **31** eighteen-and-a-half **32** "A"
33 north **34** "D" **35** Scotland Yard **36** on
37 letter **38** "D" **39** island **40** escape **41** rides
42 sixty **43** army **44** red **45** every **46** police **47** of
48 learn **49** if **50** Computer **51** each **52** men
53 eighteen-twentynine **54** new **55** women
56 handler **57** oil **58** ago **59** City **60** twenty-four
61 two **62** old **63** guns **64** enemies
65 twentysix-thousand **66** Hendon **67** evenings
68 River